GW01184857

Bible Codecrackers:

Peter & Paul

First published 2006
ISBN 1 84427 208 7

Scripture Union, 207-209 Queensway, Bletchley, Milton Keynes, MK2 2EB, England
Email: info@scriptureunion.org.uk
Website: www.scriptureunion.org.uk

Scripture Union Australia: Locked Bag 2, Central Coast Business Centre, NSW 2252 www.su.org.au

Scripture Union USA: PO Box 987, Valley Forge, PA 19482, USA www.scriptureunion.org

British Library Cataloguing in Publication Data
A catalogue record of this book is available from the British Library.

Cover design by Paul Airy (4-9-0)
Internal design and layout by Richard Jefferson
Illustrations by Pauline Adams
Printed and bound in Great Britain by Henry Ling, Dorchester.

Scripture Union is an international Christian charity working with churches in more than 130 countries providing resources to bring the good news about Jesus Christ to children, young people and families – and to encourage them to develop spiritually through the Bible and prayer.

As well as our network of volunteers, staff and associates who run holidays, church-based events and school Christian groups, we produce a wide range of publications and support those who use our resources through training programmes.

This book is dedicated to
Ella Pennells, Hannah Porter and Madeleine Egan

Contents

Introduction

We read in the Bible about the cool adventures of Jesus' best friends after he had gone to be with his Father in heaven. They carried on doing the brilliant things he'd taught them and took their God-given skills all over the place, helping and healing people as they went – but they weren't always popular. Read what some of the people involved have to say about the apostles, Jesus' special messengers. Two of the apostles we read most about were Peter and Paul.

Oh, and while you're about it, tackle some puzzles to help you remember those amazing acts. Have fun!

Are you on your toes? Answer this quiz as you read through the book. You'll need to solve the puzzles and read the bible verses to find all the answers. You can find the answers at the back of the book. Good hunting!

Quiz

1. What did Jesus do just before he went up to heaven?
2. Who lost the chance to become the new apostle?
3. What could the apostles do after the Holy Spirit came to them?
4. How many people accepted Jesus the day Peter spoke to the crowd?
5. Where was the first place the crippled man went after Peter spoke to him?
6. Who had set the apostles free from jail?
7. Whom did Stephen see as he looked into heaven?
8. What did Simon the sorcerer ask the apostles to do for him?
9. When the Ethiopian had heard the story of Jesus, what did he ask Philip to do?
10. What happened to Saul when Jesus was speaking to him?
11. When Saul could see again, what important thing happened to him?
12. Who wanted to kill Saul?
13. What happened when Peter prayed for Tabitha?
14. What did God show Peter in his vision?
15. Who freed Peter from prison?
16. What did Rhoda forget to do in her excitement?
17. What came over Elymas' eyes after Paul had spoken to him?
18. Paul said the Lord had told him to be a light for... whom?
19. What was Eunice's son called?
20. What names did the Lystra crowds call Paul and Barnabas?
21. Which laws did James suggest the Gentiles should keep?
22. What did the man in Paul's vision want him to do?
23. What happened to Paul and Silas after they were beaten?
24. What did Paul and Silas do after the jailer had washed their wounds?
25. Where did Paul and Silas go after Thessalonica?
26. What was the inscription on the altar in Athens?
27. What job did Aquila and Priscilla do?
28. What did Paul do to the 12 men in Ephesus?
29. Where did Paul go after the Ephesus riot?
30. What did Paul say he was willing to do for the Lord Jesus?
31. Who heard of a plot to kill Paul?
32. Where was Paul shipwrecked?
33. What did Paul do for the island chief, Publius?

1

Jesus goes to his Father – told by the apostle Thomas

Thomas

Since the day I first met Jesus after he'd come back to life, I've never let my faith waver again. I was so ashamed about doubting what my mates had told me.

Jesus stayed on earth for 40 days and talked to us just as before. He told us to wait for a gift God was going to send – a sort of second baptism. We couldn't think what he meant.

Our last sight of Jesus was one of the most astonishing events of my life. Solve the puzzle to find out what happened.

Can you read this odd-looking message? The clue is THREE BUT NOT THREE.

JES USR AIS EDH ISH AND
SAN DBL ESS EDH ISS PEC
IAL FRI END STH ENF LOA
TED UPW ARD STO HEA
VEN. ACL OUD HID HIM
FRO MSI GHT.

Write it out here

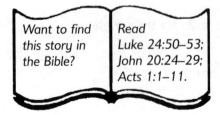

Want to find this story in the Bible?	*Read Luke 24:50–53; John 20:24–29; Acts 1:1–11.*

2

Choosing a new apostle – told by the apostle Bartholomew

Bartholomew

We were all stunned after we'd seen Jesus floating into heaven. We were still looking up when, suddenly, two men in white appeared. They looked just like anyone else but they must have been angels because one minute they weren't there, the next they were. They told us Jesus would come back to earth one day, the same way he'd left. Then they disappeared. We made our way into Jerusalem and met with Mary, her family and friends to pray.

There was a lot of talk about who would be an apostle in place of Judas Iscariot – either Justus or Matthias. We couldn't decide so we prayed, then put the two names in a box and took out one.

Who won? To find out the name of the new apostle, write down the initial letter of each of the objects shown here.

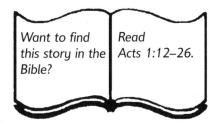

Want to find this story in the Bible? *Read Acts 1:12–26.*

3

The coming of the Holy Spirit – told by the apostle Matthias

Matthias

I could hardly believe it! I'd been chosen to be one of the famous twelve! It was very exciting, especially as Jesus had promised we would soon receive a special gift.

We had been expecting something to happen for several days. Then one day we were praying together indoors, when there was a deafening noise like a rushing wind, the strongest we'd ever heard. The wind swept through the house. We stared at each other, wondering what was happening. As I looked at my friends, I saw something unbelievable and gave a great yell.

"Peter! Philip! Thaddaeus! You're on fire!"

All my mates were shouting the same thing and I soon discovered I was on fire, too, just like the others! But the flames didn't hurt at all. What I did feel was a strange burning inside me. It was wonderful beyond words, not painful at all.

What happened next? Find out by solving the puzzle and put your answer in the box below.

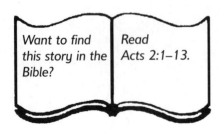

Want to find this story in the Bible?

Read Acts 2:1–13.

Here you see the apostles receiving the gift of the Holy Spirit. Can you work out the sentence written in the flames? Clue: start with the smallest flame and end with the largest.

4

Peter speaks to the crowd – told by the apostle Thaddeaus

Thaddaeus

There's no way to describe the feeling when those flames were dancing around on our heads. When the noise of the wind died down and the flames flickered out, we stood staring at each other, trying to take in what had just happened.

The silence was broken by the stampede of feet. Crowds of people arrived – and that was when we found out exactly what gift God had sent.

Many people in Jerusalem were foreigners. But, to our amazement, as we started speaking to them about God, each person heard us speak in their own language. It was as though we'd always been able to do it!

When the locals heard us speaking in other languages, they began to say we were drunk – but it was only nine o'clock in the morning. Peter gave a powerful speech and about three thousand came to Jesus that very day...

How many differences can you spot here?

Want to find this story in the Bible?

Read Acts 2:5–13,38–42.

5

Healing the lame beggar – told by a man who couldn't walk

Every day since I was little, I'd been carried to the Beautiful Gate near the Temple and set down on the ground to beg. People were always going in and out of the Temple and some of them would toss me a coin. And that was my life for years – until I met two of the Teacher's friends.

I'd heard of Jesus but had never believed the stories. How could he make the blind see and the lame walk? It didn't seem possible to me.

So, when two of Jesus' followers came to the Temple, I didn't expect anything apart from a few coins. I had the shock of my life when the one called Peter looked me straight in the eye and said, "I have no money but, in the name of Jesus Christ, I order you to get up and walk."

My first reaction was "Really?" But then...

To find out what happened, solve the puzzle. By the way, I'm sorry I ever doubted. Jesus is the greatest!

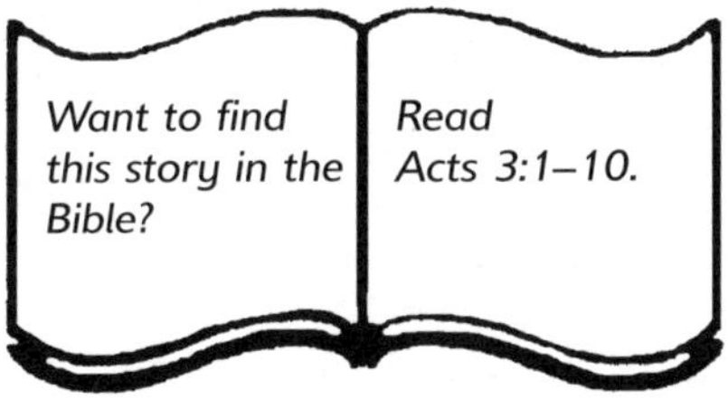
Want to find this story in the Bible?
Read Acts 3:1–10.

Cross out the first letter of the message below, then put a circle round the next letter. Now cross out the next two letters and circle the next. Keep doing that: crossing out first one, and circling the next, then crossing out two letters and circling the next, right through the puzzle. The circled letters in order will tell you what happened as soon as Peter had spoken to the lame man.

A T R G H T E N M L E A H J M T E B N M O A V D N T S B
N T W O D F O P D F G U E P Z X A R N Y H D H S E F T T
A F G R E T U I E D D O P T D O C V W R A S D L J K . S S H
X E G R W Y E M M N U T P P I L N R E T G O H J T M H Y
T E Q T R E E B M G G P N L U Y E, I P L L R O A Y U I K S F
T I H N M N G C G X Z O F D.

Write the circled letters on the steps of the Beautiful Gate. The first two words are done for you.

6

Peter and John are arrested – twice! – told by Alexander

Alexander

Bet you've never heard of me. I'm a relative of Annas, the high priest. Along with members of my family and other Sanhedrin Council officials, I've been watching a group of followers of Jesus of Nazareth. Despite everything we've done, his friends have succeeded in stealing his body and telling anyone who'd listen that he'd "come alive again from the dead".

Two of his followers, Peter and John, were going through the city, spreading rumours about Jesus being the Jewish Messiah, the person God promised to send to his people. Of course, we had to stop that, so when the Sadducees had the men arrested, we stepped in.

We questioned Peter and John but couldn't hold them for long – they hadn't done anything wrong. They stuck to their stupid Messiah story, but we told them to stop spreading the rumours and let them go.

But they just carried on where they'd left off. So we arrested them again. This time, we threw them into jail under strict security. But the following morning... find out what happened by using our story wheel.

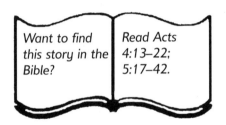

Want to find this story in the Bible?

Read Acts 4:13–22; 5:17–42.

Start with the letter in the centre, then read the letters in the wheel in clockwise order, starting at the middle circle and working outwards. Write down the letters as you go. Always start the next circle by reading the letter to the right of the bold line first.

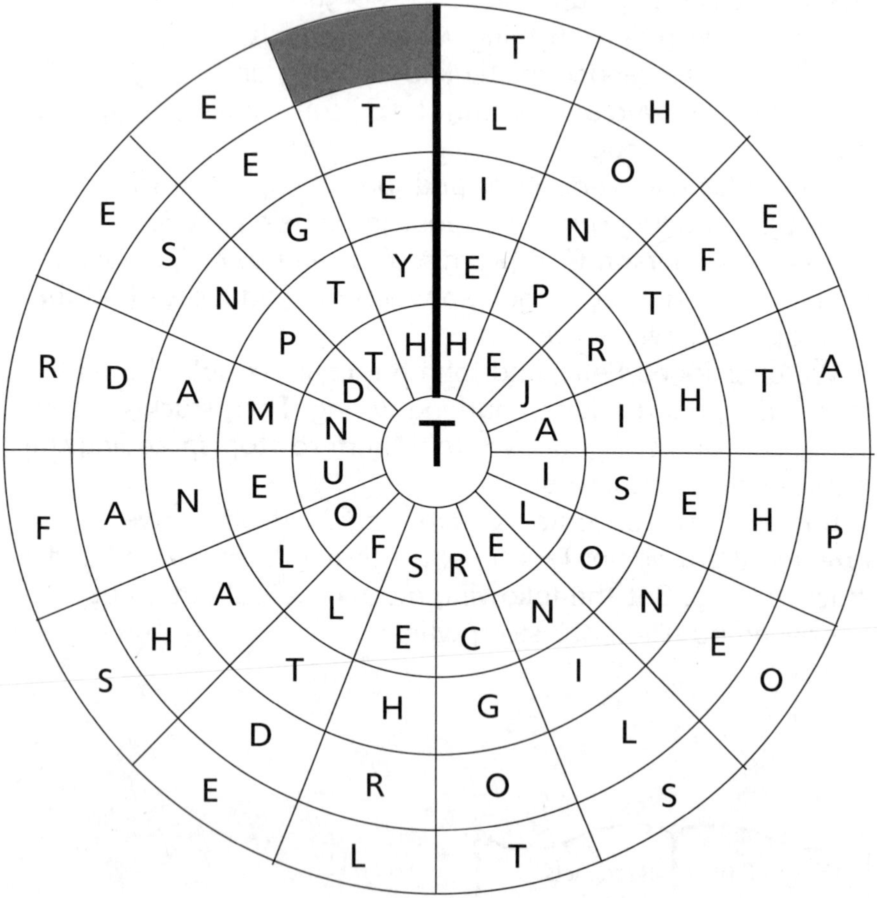

7

The stoning of Stephen – told by Saul

Saul

It's hard to believe how much I doubted Jesus! God forgive me! I have a new name now, but in those days, I was called Saul. I used to think I was very important. Nothing I liked better than sorting out those troublemakers who were blaspheming in the name of Jesus.

I'd come to Jerusalem to be trained in Jewish law. I was outraged when I heard that Stephen, a follower of Jesus, was saying Jesus had changed the laws of Moses. We had to get rid of Stephen. We threw him out of Jerusalem and stoned him to death. I didn't chuck any stones myself; I just held everyone's coats while they did the dirty deed. But I cheered them. Now I am so ashamed.

Do you know what an anagram is? It's a word with the letters jumbled up. Sort out all the anagrams in the stones to find out what Stephen cried out to God.

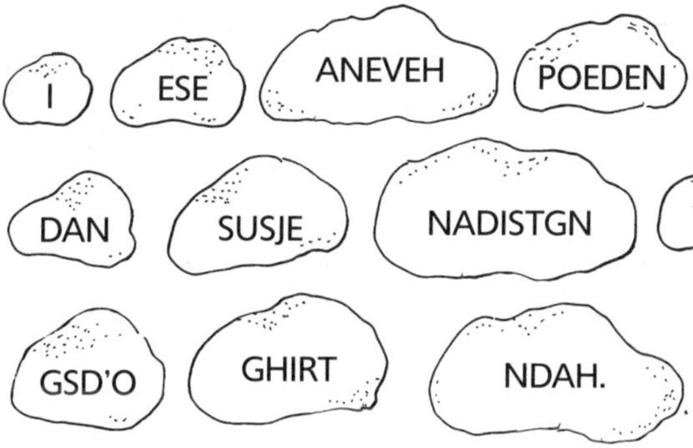

Want to find this story in the Bible?

Read Acts 6:8–15; 7:54 – 8:1–3.

8

The apostles visit Samaria – told by Simon the sorcerer

Simon

I was well known for my magic powers around here. Local Samaritans just loved me and called me "The Great Power". But when the Jewish preacher called Philip turned up in our town, I thought he had something very special.

Philip was one of Jesus' followers. He told us that through Jesus' power, he could do miracles and healings. I was so amazed with the fantastic things Philip was doing in Jesus' name that I asked to be baptised, as a sign that I believed in Jesus.

Then Peter and John (two more of Jesus' followers) showed up in Samaria. They started laying hands on people. Instantly they received God's Holy Spirit! Naturally, I wanted that power, too, and because I was used to being paid for my magic tricks, I offered Peter a generous sum.

I was so surprised when Peter got very angry with me. He told me I didn't love God as I ought to and that I was full of bitterness and sin. My first instinct was to hit him but something stopped me. What do you think I did instead?

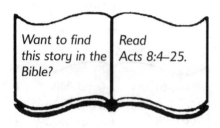

Want to find this story in the Bible?

Read Acts 8:4–25.

Find out by looking at some pretty odd writing.

▽↓↘⇕↔ ⇨▽↗⇨⇦ ◀↑⇨ ⇨▲⇕▽◀↙⇨▽

_ _ _ _ _   _ _ _ _ _   _ _ _   _ _ _ _ _ _ _ _

◀⇕ ▲△⇨◢ ←⇕△ ↑↓↘ ▽⇕ ◀↑⇨◀

_ _   _ _ _ _   _ _ _   _ _ _   _ _   _ _ _ _

↑⇨ ▷⇕▶↙⇦ ⇦⇨ △↓→↑◀ ↓↔

_ _   _ _ _ _ _   _ _   _ _ _ _ _   _ _

→⇕⇦'▽ ⇨◢⇨▽.

_ _ _'_   _ _ _ _.

Here is the  *to decode the message.*

a	b	c	d	e	f	g	h	i	j	k	l	m
⇨	⇦	⇨	⇦	⇨	←	→	↑	↓	↖	↗	↙	↘

n	o	p	q	r	s	t	u	v	w	x	y	z
↔	⇕	▲	▼	△	▽	◀	▶	◁	▷	◣	◢	◤

9

An Ethiopian official reads Isaiah – told by the apostle Philip

Philip

I was really surprised when an angel told me to go on the old southbound Gaza road, out of Jerusalem. I was used to God asking me to do unexpected things and knew it would soon become clear.

I was walking along when I heard the clatter of a horse's hooves coming up behind me. The horse was pulling a rather smart carriage. The Lord told me to stay close to it. It's hard for someone on foot to keep up with a carriage, but God gave me the strength and speed I needed. I saw that the carriage had the crest of the Ethiopian royal family. The well-dressed man in the carriage looked very important. (He turned out to be treasurer to the Ethiopian queen.) He was reading out loud from the Jewish scriptures and was struggling to understand a prophecy of Isaiah.

"I wish I had someone to explain it to me," he sighed. I soon found myself sitting beside him, talking about the passage he'd been reading and telling him the good news of Jesus Christ. Hundreds of years ago, Isaiah had written about the coming of Jesus

Amazingly, this very important man believed what I told him and asked to be baptised.

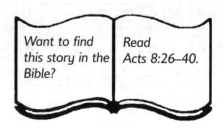

Want to find this story in the Bible? *Read Acts 8:26–40.*

Find the route Philip took to meet the official.

10

Saul meets Jesus – told by Saul's companion

Saul, my commander, hated the followers of Jesus and instructed us to search for them in Damascus. We were told to arrest any followers we found.

Everything was going smoothly as we marched towards Damascus. Suddenly there was a flash of bright light – not lightning because we weren't in a storm – and to our horror, we saw Saul fall to the ground. We heard a clear, strong voice coming from nowhere.

"Saul, Saul! Why are you persecuting me?"

"Who are you?" gasped Saul, terrified.

"I am Jesus, the person you are persecuting," said the voice.

We all shook with fright.

Read this story in the Bible then circle whether the following statements are true or false:

Saul was told to stay where he was. True/False

His companions did not hear anything. True/False

Saul saw a bright light. True/False

Saul led them to Damascus. True/False

He did not eat or drink for three days. True/False

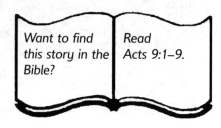

Want to find this story in the Bible? *Read Acts 9:1–9.*

11

Saul believes in Jesus – told by Ananias

Ananias

You can imagine that I listened carefully when I had a vision from the Lord.

"Ananias," he said, "go to Judas' house in Straight Street and ask for Saul of Tarsus. He's had a bit of a bad experience. He's expecting you to visit him."

It turned out that this man had been made blind on his way from Jerusalem to Damascus. He was hoping I'd lay hands on him to heal him.

I wasn't at all keen on this job. "Lord," I said, anxiously, "I've heard of this man. He's done dreadful things to your people in Jerusalem and he's only come to Damascus to create more trouble. Even if he's blind, he's still a force to be reckoned with. Must I go?"

The Lord insisted. He told me he'd chosen Saul to serve him in a special way which would be quite amazing to see!

I found Saul. He didn't seem very terrifying – just a rather small man, upset and confused by his blindness. I put my hands on his shoulders and told him God had sent me so that he'd see again and be filled with the Holy Spirit.

Find out what happened next.

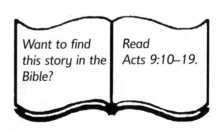

Want to find this story in the Bible? *Read Acts 9:10–19.*

The words below all fit into the framework – all you have to do is to decide which word goes where. We've put in a few letters to help you discover what happened when Ananias laid hands on Saul.

2 letters: HE HE HE UP

3 letters: AND HAD HIS WAS SEE

4 letters: BACK CAME EYES FELL FISH FROM LIKE

5 letters: AFTER COULD EATEN SAUL'S STOOD

6 letters: SCALES

8 letters: BAPTISED STRENGTH

9 letters: SOMETHING

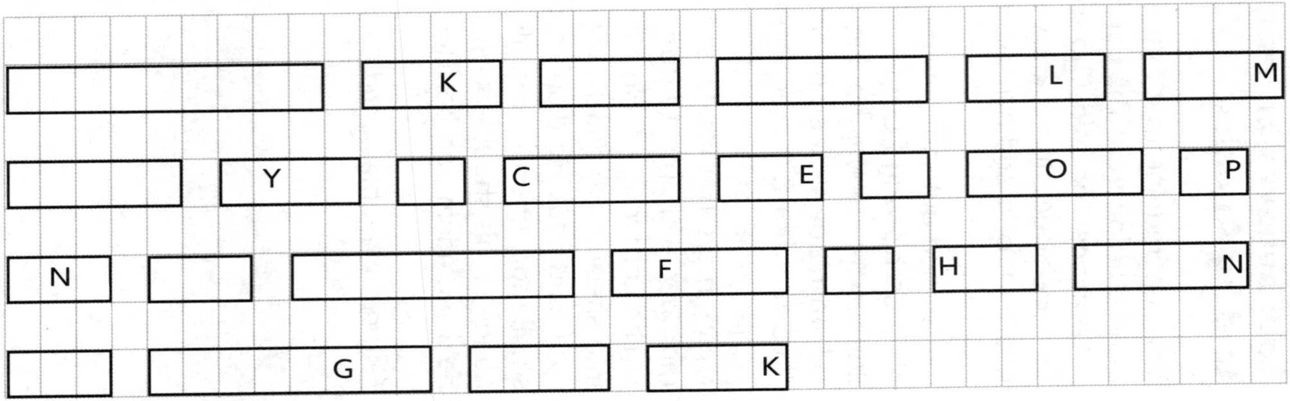

12

Saul joins the apostles – told by the apostle James

James

When the news broke that Saul of Tarsus was now a believer, I was sure it was a trick. But no, it seemed Saul had had a life-changing experience. Jesus had spoken to him and now he really wanted to serve God. What a turnaround!

Damascus was buzzing. Could this really be the man who'd been so determined to imprison Jesus' followers? Saul preached so powerfully that Jesus was indeed the Messiah. Some non-believing Jews planned to kill Saul. They watched the city gates carefully to stop him leaving Damascus, but Saul came up with a cunning plan!

Fill in the missing vowels: a, e, i, o, u.

_ne n_ght S_ _l's f_ll_w_rs t_ _k h_m _nd l_t

h_m d_wn thr_ _gh _n _p_n_ng _n th_ w_ll

l_w_r_ng h_m _n _ b_sk_t.

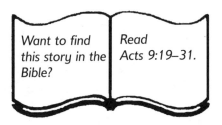

Want to find this story in the Bible?

Read Acts 9:19–31.

Join up the dots to see how Saul escaped.

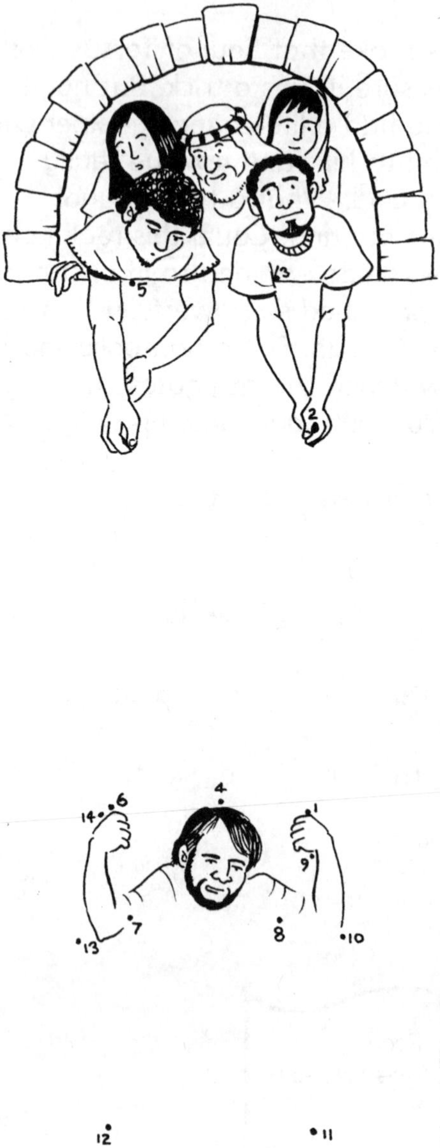

13

Peter heals in the name of Jesus – told by Aeneas

Aeneas

We'd heard so much about the fisherman Peter. He was one of Jesus' best friends. I heard he was visiting Lydda, my hometown. Would he be able to heal me, just as Jesus had healed so many other paralysed people? I'd been unable to get out of bed for the past eight years, a hard thing for an active man.

My friends made sure Peter came to see me. He took one look at me and said Jesus would cure me.

"Get up and make your bed," he commanded – and I did. Just like that.

I couldn't let this great man out of my sight. I followed him around Lydda as he told everyone about the wonderful things Jesus had done.

One day, a message came from nearby Joppa. Tabitha, a good woman who always helped everyone, had died. Her family had sent for Peter. Peter rushed off to Joppa. A crowd of people followed. I went, too!

Find out what happened there.

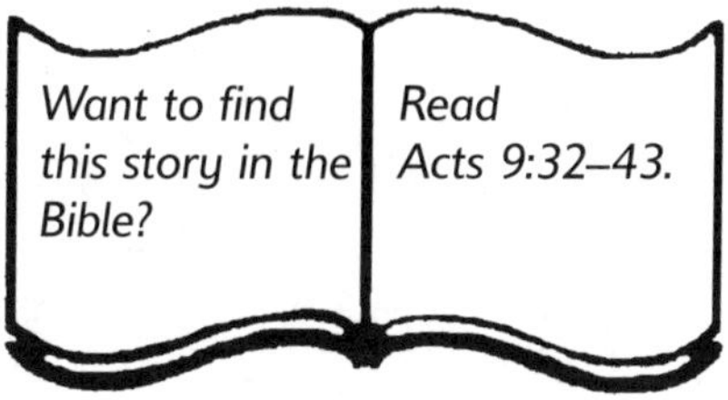
Want to find this story in the Bible?
Read Acts 9:32–43.

Write down the letters shown in the squares in the order 1,2,3,4 to find out the strange thing Jesus said. Do the first square first, then the next and so on.

1 2
4 3

P	E	R	S	T	A	T	H	O	U	E	R	W	A	N	E	D	O	A	N	R	A
E	T	N	E	L	L	M	E	N	R	A	S	K	Y	T	L	N	W	P	D	E	Y

D	T	N	H	A	I	A	B	H	A	T	U	A	B	H	A	E	N	H	E	Y	E	N	D
E	H	S	E	T	D	T	I	E	G	T	P	T	I	P	O	D	E	E	R	A	S	E	P

T	E	E	L	D	H	S	T	D	U	E	C	S	E	T	H	M	A	P	E	L	E	J	O	A	B
H	R	E	P	R	E	N	A	B	P	U	A	F	O	S	I	Y	N	P	O	N	I	P	P	C	E

A	M	E	L	V	E
B	E	E	I	S	R

_ _ _ _ _ / _ _ _ _ / _ _ _ / _ _ _ / _ _ _ _ _ _ _ _ /

_ _ _ _ , / _ _ _ _ _ / _ _ _ _ / _ _ _ / _ _ _ _ _ _ . /

_ _ _ _ / _ _ / _ _ _ _ / “ _ _ _ _ _ _ _ ! / _ _ _ /

_ _ !” / _ _ _ _ _ _ _ / _ _ _ _ _ _ / _ _ _ / _ _ _ _ /

_ _ _ / _ _ _ _ _ / _ _ _ _ _ _ / _ _ _ / _ _ _ _ _ / _ _ . /

_ _ _ _ _ _ _ / _ _ / _ _ _ _ , / _ _ _ _ / _ _ _ _ _ _ /

_ _ / _ _ _ _ _ / _ _ _ _ _ _ / _ _ _ _ _ _ _ _ _ .

14

Peter has a vision and some visitors – told by Simon the tanner

Simon

Peter came to stay with me while he was in Joppa. I'm a tanner, working with leather (that's animal skin) – it's a bit smelly. Peter didn't seem to care – but then, he'd been a fisherman so he was used to smells.

Peter liked to pray on the roof in the sunshine. One day, just as I was about to call him down for the midday meal, three Roman soldiers arrived at my gate. I never felt comfortable with Romans. I was relieved to find they were some of Captain Cornelius' men. He was well known for being a good religious man.

I found out later that Cornelius had had a vision of an angel, who'd told him where to find Peter. And would you believe it? At the very moment the men arrived, Peter was having a vision, too, right there on my roof. (To find out about Peter's vision, solve the puzzle on page 28.)

"I have to go to Caesarea," Peter announced. "Cornelius wants me to tell him about Jesus."

The Romans stayed the night and next morning they set off for Caesarea with Peter.

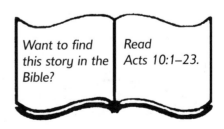

Want to find this story in the Bible?

Read Acts 10:1–23.

Remember what anagrams are? We had some earlier – words with the letters jumbled up. Some of the words below are anagrams, others aren't. Sort them out to discover what Peter saw in his dream and write your answer in the sheet.

OGD SHOWED REEPT ALL KINDS OF SNAILMA AND DRIBS. HE TOLD PETER TO LILK AND TAE THEM – BUT PETER REGAUD. WEJS HAVE STRICT WALS ABOUT WHAT THEY CAN EAT AND THE YAW ANIMALS MUST BE DILKEL.

"I CAN'T AET THOSE!" HE SAID, "I'VE VEENR EATEN ANYTHING NUNCLEA."

"DON'T CONSIDER GHINYTAN UNCLEAN IF I NOW TELL YOU IT'S DOGO TO EAT," SAID ODG.

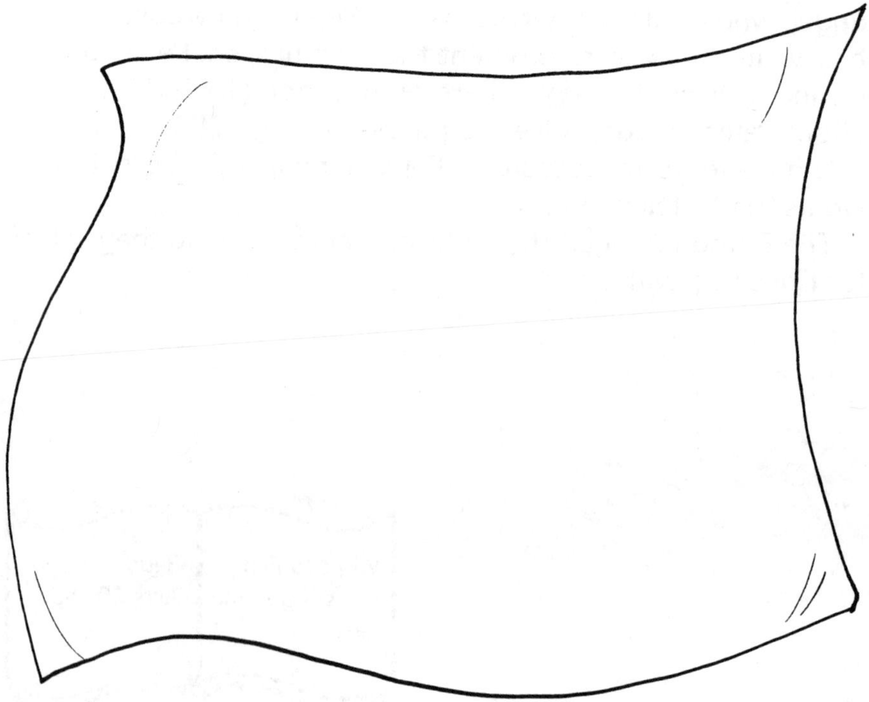

15

James is killed and Peter is arrested – told by the apostle John

John

This has been a good year. The number of believers has been growing every day. There are now thousands of us in many places across the country. Even Gentiles, not just Jews, believe in Jesus.

But it has been a bad year, too, especially for my family. King Herod was against the followers of Jesus. He turned his attention to my brother James. I can hardly bear to write it. James was murdered. My family are all devastated, and so are the rest of Jesus' followers. Of course, we know that James is in a better place, with Jesus himself!

Herod followed up the murder by arresting Peter. We prayed for Peter, so, we knew the Lord would help.

Find out how – solve the puzzle.

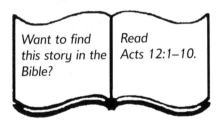

Want to find this story in the Bible? *Read Acts 12:1–10.*

To work out this puzzle, you'll need this number code.

Z	Y	X	W	V	U	T	S	R	Q	P	O	N	M	L	K	J	I	H	G	F	E	D	C	B	A
1	2	3	4	5	6	7	8	9	10	11	12	13	14	15	16	17	18	19	20	21	22	23	24	25	26

26 13/ 26 13 20 22 15/ 4 12 16 22/ 11 22 7 22 9/26 13 23/

19 18 8/24 19 26 18 13 8/21 22 15 15/12 21 21/7 19 22/

26 13 20 22 15/15 22 23/19 18 14/ 7 19 9 12 6 20 19/

7 19 22/11 9 18 8 12 13/20 26 7 22 8/7 12/8 26 21 22 7 2.

Write the answer in the blocks.

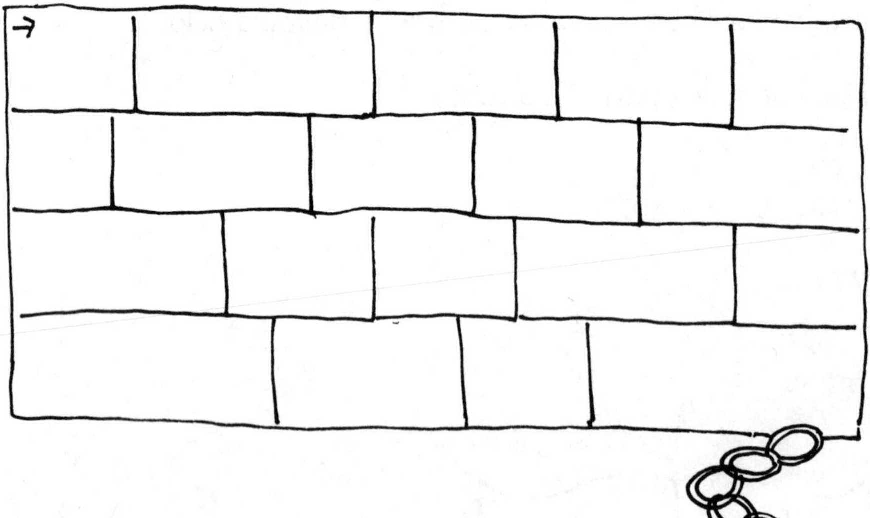

16

Peter visits his friends - told by Rhoda

Rhoda

We were all so upset. First, King Herod had James killed. Then, Peter was thrown into prison.

Mary, the woman I work for, is always very practical. As soon as she heard about Peter's arrest, she sent me and the other servants all over town to invite every believer to her house to pray.

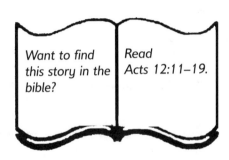

"We can pray alone," she said, briskly, "but Jesus said that when people gather in his name, he'll be with them in a special way."

People were praying together so loudly that I only just caught the sound of knocking. I wanted to go on praying but it was my job to answer the door.

As I peered through the grille, my heart leapt. Peter was standing there. I couldn't believe it. I ran shrieking to my mistress. (I didn't think to open the door.)

"It's Peter! He's not in prison – he's right here on the doorstep!"

Strangely enough, no one believed me.

Want to find this story in the bible? *Read Acts 12:11–19.*

This isn't exactly a puzzle. They're words to reflect on. That's the clue.

Rhoda was so
excited she forgot
to let Peter in!

Peter kept knocking until
the door was opened. He
told his friends how God
had brought him out of
prison, gave them a
message for the other
apostles, and then went
away to hide.

17

Paul meets the governor of Cyprus – told by Sergius Paulus

Sergius

I'm the governor of the island of Cyprus and was delighted when I heard Saul had arrived in the port of Salamis. That's to the east of the island. I wanted to know why he was so keen on Jesus, when for years he'd been against him.

I finally met him, along with Barnabas and John Mark, in my hometown of Paphos on the west coast.

We were deep in discussion when Elymas the magician interrupted us. He didn't like the idea that I might believe in Jesus. Paul looked straight at him and said, "You son of the devil! You are full of all kinds of evil tricks!" To my astonishment, Paul told Elymas that God would blind him there and then for his evil ways.

Want to hear what happened? Sort out this puzzle.

Choose the right word from the ones given here in brackets to discover what happened when Paul told Elymas he had an evil spirit. Cross out the other two words in each set of brackets to tell the story.

(Paphos, Paulus, Elymas) felt a dark (mist, bird, tree) cover his (hand, ears, eyes) and (skipped, walked, danced) about trying to find (elephants, someone, footballs) to lead him by the (nose, hair, hand). The (governor, greengrocer, blacksmith) was amazed and believed in (Jesus, Satan, Barnabas) because of Paul's (teaching, singing, jogging).

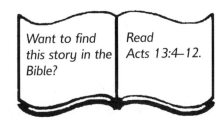

Want to find this story in the Bible? *Read Acts 13:4–12.*

18

The first journey begins – told by Barnabas

Barnabas

John Mark and I were very pleased to be travelling with Paul to tell others about Jesus.

Wherever we went, we explained to everyone that Jesus was the long awaited Jewish Messiah. "Messiah" means "The Anointed One".

We left Antioch in Syria, and went to Salamis and Paphos in Cyprus, and Perga in Pamphylia. From there, Paul and I went on to Antioch in Pisidia. Many people came to hear Paul's message but local Jewish leaders were angry that he was preaching to Gentiles, people who weren't Jews. Solve the puzzle to find out what he said to them.

Paul told them that the Lord said:

Want to find this story in the Bible? Read Acts 13:13–18; 44–52.

19

Amazing things happen in Lystra – told by Eunice

Eunice

As soon as I heard Paul had arrived in Lystra, I rushed off to hear him. I was brought up a devout Jew, but I married someone who is not a Jew. My Greek husband and I gave our son a Greek name: Timothy.

Timothy came with me to hear Paul speak in the synagogue about Jesus. We were both bowled over by what we heard. Timothy believed straight away and became a Christian.

Our neighbour believed, too, for an amazing reason. He'd been lame from birth and had to be carried to the synagogue every week. He listened intently to Paul, never moving a muscle. Suddenly, Paul looked straight at him and said in a loud voice, "Stand up!"

You could have heard a pin drop. Then our neighbour jumped up and began walking around – just like that! Astounding!

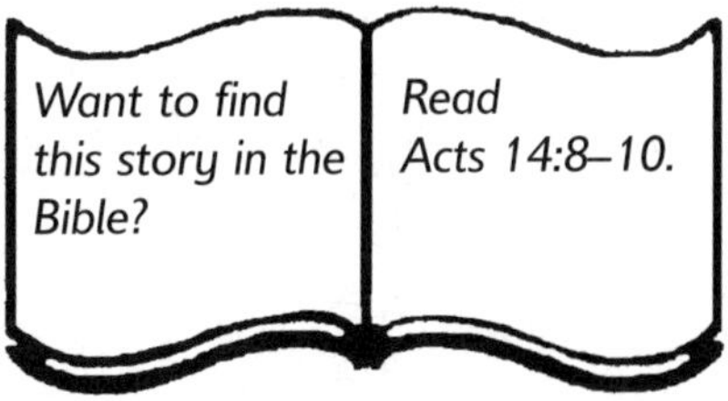

Want to find this story in the Bible?
Read Acts 14:8–10.

Can you find the two pictures that are exactly the same?

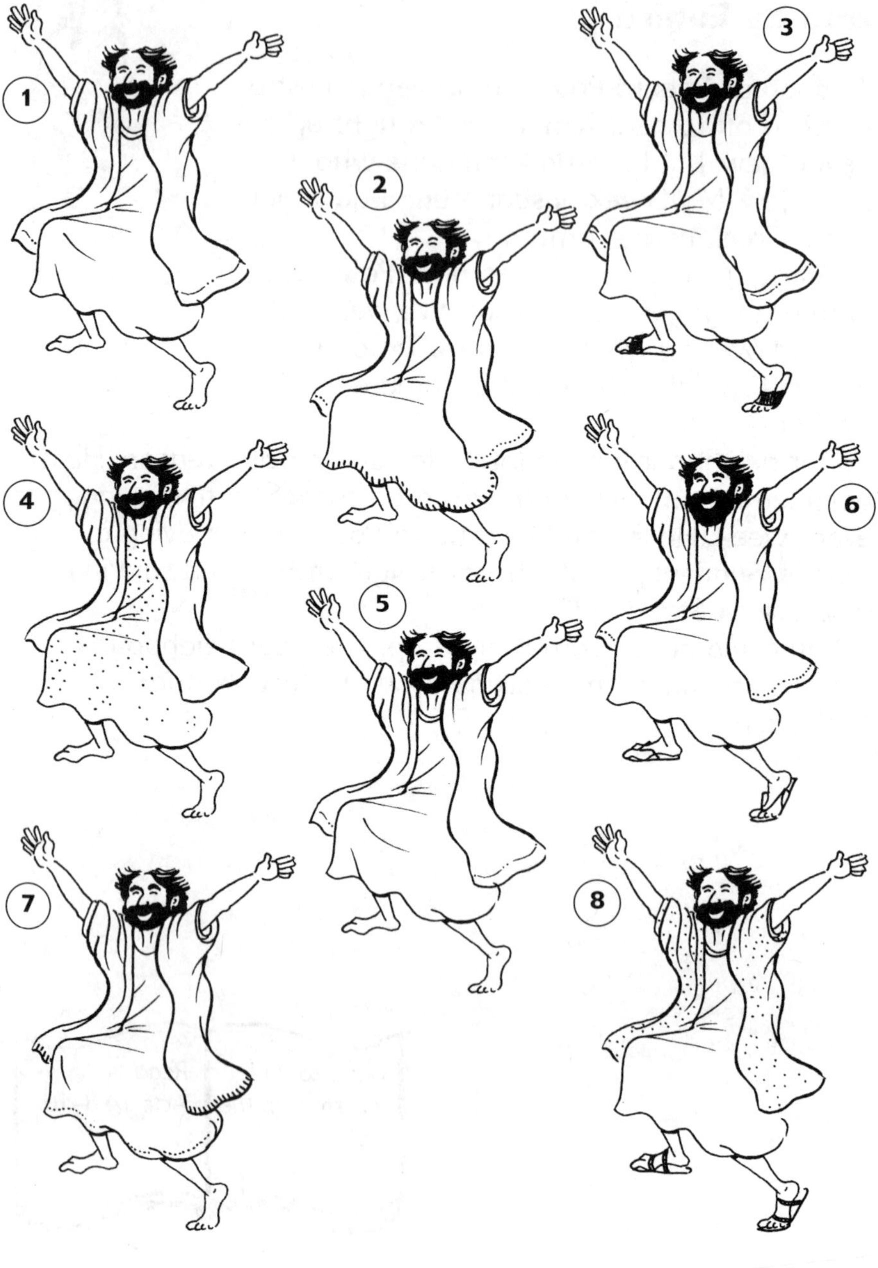

20

The first journey continues – told by Lois

Lois

After the lame man was healed, the crowd thought Paul and Barnabas were gods. They named them Hermes and Zeus! Paul and Barnabas were furious. This was the last thing they wanted!

"We're human, just like the rest of you," Paul said firmly. "You must worship God the creator of all – and only him!"

The crowd didn't want to believe Paul. They threw stones at him, leaving him for dead. We waited anxiously until Paul became conscious again. Then we took him home with us for the night. Next day, he and Barnabas escaped to Derbe, where they helped many people become followers of Jesus.

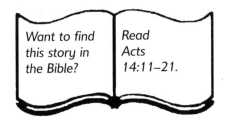

Want to find this story in the Bible? *Read Acts 14:11–21.*

Find out what Paul said to encourage these new believers by taking time to look back...

".doG fo modgnik eht retne ot selbuort
ynam hguorht ssap tsum eW"

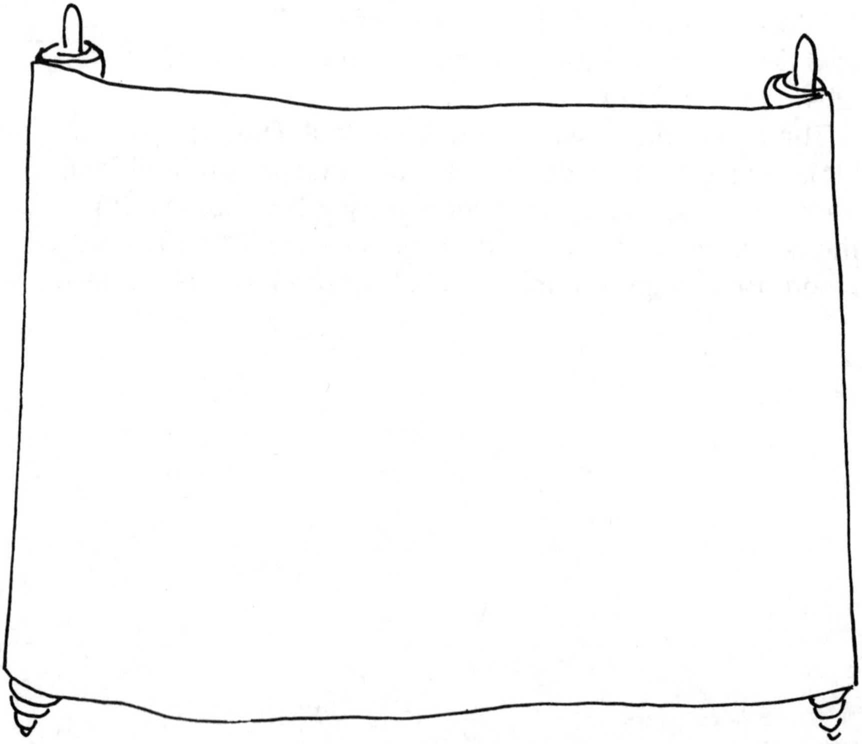

Write the information in the scroll.

21

Paul speaks to the Jerusalem church leaders – told by Judas Barsabbas

Judas B

My name's Judas Barsabbas and I am a member of the Jerusalem Church Council. Yesterday, Paul and Barnabas arrived. We were excited to hear about how the Gentiles were turning to God. But then someone stood up and said the Gentiles had to follow Jewish laws if they were Christians. These laws were about things like the type of food we can eat.

We talked about this for ages. Finally Peter stood up and spoke very clearly. He said there was no need to burden Gentile believers to keep Jewish laws. God had shown he accepted them by giving them his Holy Spirit, just like Jews.

"We believe and are saved by the grace of the Lord Jesus, just as they are," he stated firmly.

Everyone was quiet as Barnabas and Paul reminded us of all the miracles and wonders God had done for the Gentiles. James came up with a very sensible suggestion.

Solve the puzzle to hear what it was.

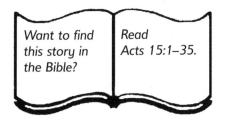

Want to find this story in the Bible?

Read Acts 15:1–35.

Put the 12 listed words into the right places in "The Gentile Rap".

food prophets Jesus Gather James do Gentiles worship above Jewish baptised letter

The Gentile Rap

________ said, "_______ round and listen to me.

The words of the _________ all agree

With Peter's words. So let's write a______

Telling those _________ they had better

Keep just a few of the _______ laws

About behaviour and _____ because

That'll keep us happy – and _____, too –

So that is all they'll have to ___,

As long as they're all _________ in love

And _________ only our God ______."

22

The second journey begins – told by Silas

Silas

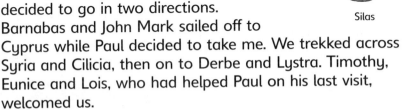

Paul and Barnabas both wanted to travel to check on how all the groups of new believers were getting on. The problem was that Barnabas wanted to take John Mark with them but, for some reason, Paul disagreed.

The problem was solved when we decided to go in two directions. Barnabas and John Mark sailed off to Cyprus while Paul decided to take me. We trekked across Syria and Cilicia, then on to Derbe and Lystra. Timothy, Eunice and Lois, who had helped Paul on his last visit, welcomed us.

Everywhere we went, we read out the letter from the Jerusalem Church Council and told the believers to do what it said. Everywhere we went, churches grew stronger and stronger. It was a fantastic trip.

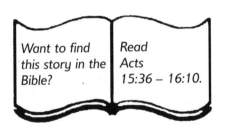

Want to find this story in the Bible?

Read Acts 15:36 – 16:10.

Our next stop was decided for us in a most peculiar way. Interested? Try this puzzle.

The first two words are done for you. Can you work out how the code works?

PUHDVSOIHSLEAAWSEGNHMOEOAEOIADEPS
ALAAIINNISEPMNABGIGICMTMCDNANHLU

Write the answer here:

Paul had _ ______ __ ___ _____. _ ___

___ ________ ___, "____ __ __________

___ ____ __."

23

Paul and Silas preach in Macedonia – told by Timothy

Timothy

I never thought Paul and Silas would end up in prison! I travelled with them to Philippi, a Roman colony in Macedonia, for a few days. There we met a slave-girl who was paid to tell people's fortunes. When she saw us, she screamed at the top of her voice, "These men are servants of God! They're telling you how to be saved." That was true, of course, but it was an evil spirit that made her say it. She screamed for days and days. Paul sorted it out but, as a result, he and Silas were thrown into jail. Want to know how? You know what to do...

Solve this word search, crossing out each word as you find it. Now write down the remaining letters in order to find out the charge against Paul and Silas. Their accusers said they were – what?

BEATEN FORTUNE FURIOUS MONEY PAUL
PRISON ROMANS SILAS SLAVE

P	F	O	R	T	U	N	E
R	U	T	O	R	O	B	U
I	R	B	M	O	N	E	Y
S	I	L	A	S	L	A	P
O	O	E	N	M	A	T	A
N	U	K	S	E	R	E	U
S	S	L	A	V	E	N	L

Want to find this story in the Bible? *Read Acts 16:10–24.*

24

Paul and Silas in and out of prison – told by their jailer

I am just an ordinary man with a nasty job, a jailer!

But an extraordinary thing has happened to me.

It began the other night, when two men, who were preaching about Jesus, were thrown into my jail. Their clothes were all ripped. They were bruised and bleeding from being beaten. I pushed them into the cell and tied their feet between blocks of wood. But I was amazed to hear them singing songs to God as though they were happy! The other prisoners listened, completely surprised.

Suddenly, the whole place was shaken with a massive earthquake. All the prisoners' chains broke loose. There was nothing to stop them escaping. I felt really sick inside. The authorities would be sure to blame me. I was so scared. I thought of killing myself. Then I heard Paul shout, "Don't do it! We're all here!"

I found a light and led the prisoners to safety. It was then that I surprised myself. I asked Paul what I had to do to be like him.

He said, "Have faith in Jesus!"

I asked Paul if he would baptise me along with my family. He did it that very night.

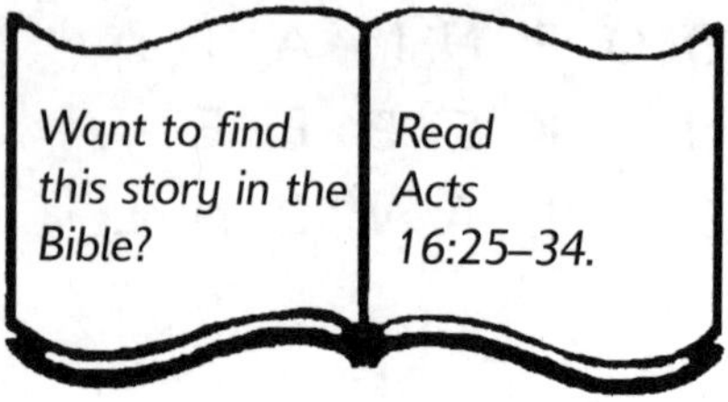
Want to find this story in the Bible?
Read Acts 16:25–34.

Can you find eight differences between these two pictures of Paul in prison?

25

Paul and Silas preach in Thessalonica – told by Jason

Jason

Paul and Silas were staying with me in my house in Thessalonica. They had just gone out for some food when I heard a noise outside. A crowd of hooligans stormed into my house and demanded to know where Paul and Silas had gone. When they couldn't find them, they dragged me and some others to the town authorities. They accused us of being troublemakers. We were only released after paying some money!

As soon as it was dark, we sent Paul and Silas away to Berea. Despite this opposition to Paul's message, many Greeks have come to believe, including many women. That's great news!

Look carefully at the words below to find out the message Paul had about Jesus.

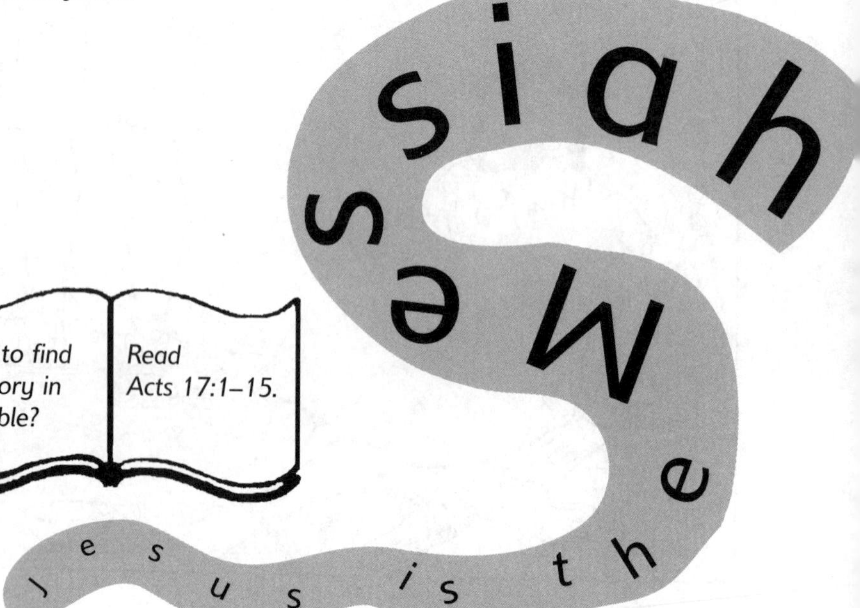

Want to find this story in the Bible?

Read Acts 17:1–15.

26

Paul speaks about idols in Athens – told by Damaris

Damaris

There are far too many stone statues in our city. The Jewish law forbids it. But then there are not many Jews in Athens. I'm a well-educated Athenian woman. I used to be taken in by all the gold and silver stuff myself. We Greeks have some really beautiful statues, sculpted by famous craftsmen. Our greatest thinkers debate about them. They spend all day talking about every subject under the sun.

There's one particular altar where they love to meet to debate. It has an inscription: "To an Unknown God". I'd often wondered about this unknown god and I was really pleased when Paul arrived and explained who he was. At last it all made sense!

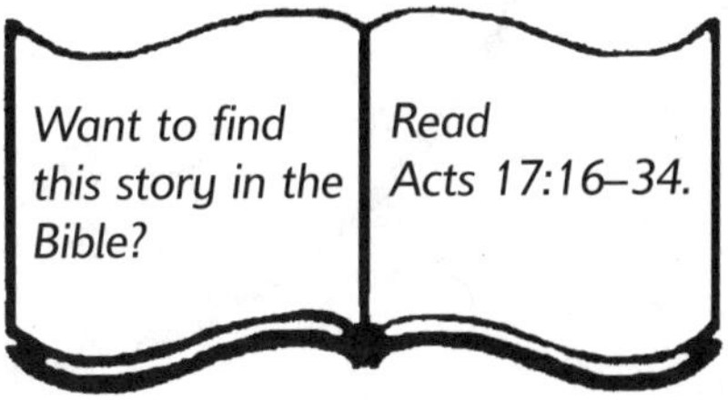
Want to find this story in the Bible?
Read Acts 17:16–34.

In this message, BKQXZ are unwanted letters. Cross out all those letters to reveal what Paul said to Damaris about God.

G K Q O D, Z B K K Q W X Z H Q Q Z O M A Q D
Z K E K Q X T Z H E K K X W Q Z K O R B Z L D X
K A Q N Q B K D Z E Q V E X R X X X Y T K Z B H
I X K N G X B Z I K Q B N I Z X T, Q X I S K K L Z X
O Q B R X Z D X K O K B F Q Z H X Q E A V X Z E
N B K A X X N D Q Z Z E K Q A Z X R T X H K .

Write the message in the globe below:

27

Paul returns to Corinth – told by Priscilla

Priscilla

My husband, Aquila, and I live in Corinth. My husband is a Jewish Christian. We used to live in Rome until the Emperor Claudius turned all the Jews out of the city. A group of believers often meets at our house to pray and worship God. We have recently welcomed Paul as a special guest. He has helped us a lot because he earns his living by making tents, just as we do.

Write below as many words as you can make out of the word "Tentmaker"

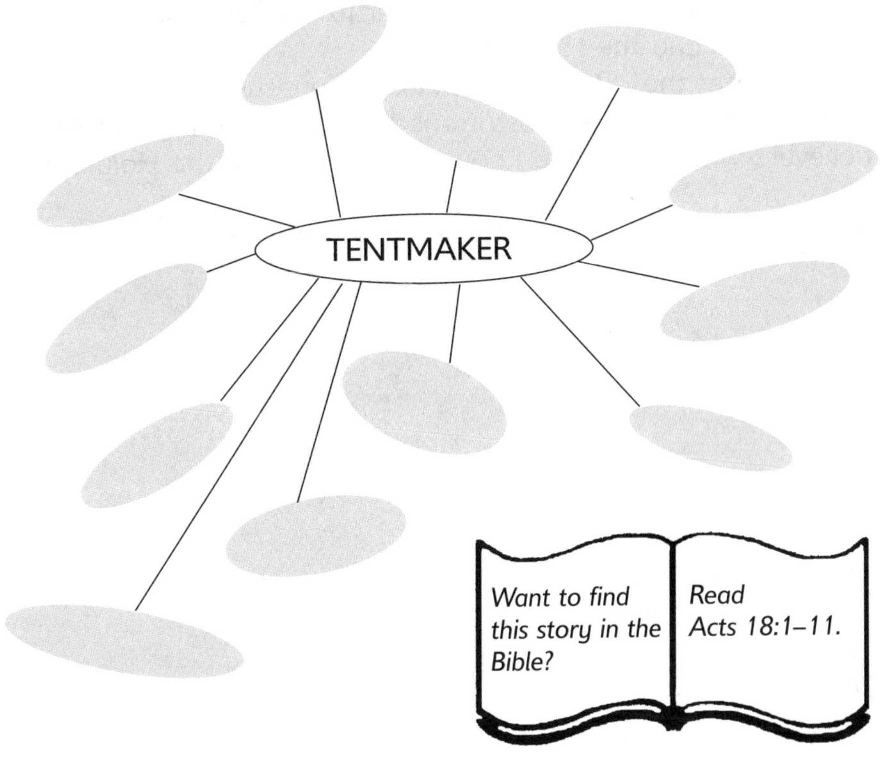
TENTMAKER
Want to find this story in the Bible?
Read Acts 18:1–11.

28

The third journey begins – told by Aquila

Aquilla

Priscilla and I closed down our tent-making business and went with our good friend Paul to Syria. We settled in Ephesus while Paul travelled around telling people the good news about Jesus. Many more people became followers of Jesus in Caesarea, Antioch, Galatia and Phrygia. The word was spreading!

While Paul was away, Apollos, a very clever Jew from Alexandria, came to see us. He could quote the Jewish scriptures from start to finish. He had heard about Jesus but only knew about John's type of baptising. We took him home with us and told him everything Paul had taught us about Jesus and the Holy Spirit.

Soon after that, Paul came back to Ephesus. We were so pleased to see him! Almost immediately, he ran into twelve believers who wanted to know about receiving the Holy Spirit.

Solve the puzzle to find out what happened next.

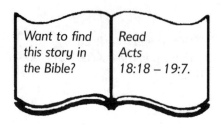

Want to find this story in the Bible? *Read Acts 18:18 – 19:7.*

This bookshelf is a bit of a mess! Can you tidy it up by putting the shortest book at the left-hand end of the shelf and the others in size order after it, finishing with the tallest book on the right? Write the new sentence in the empty bookshelf.

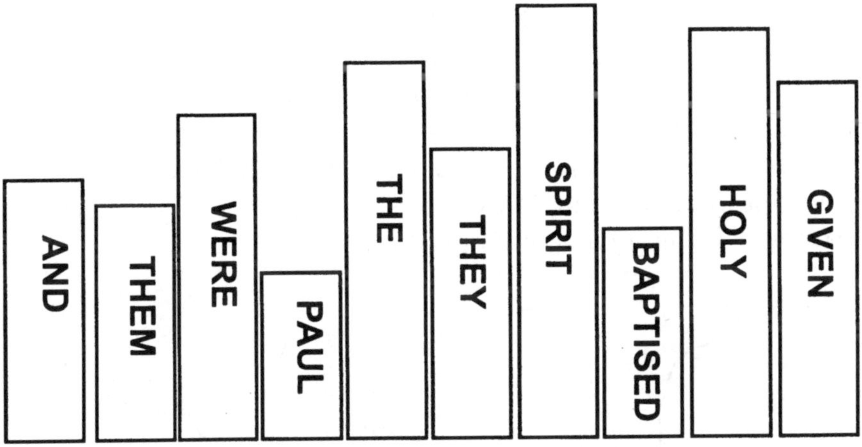

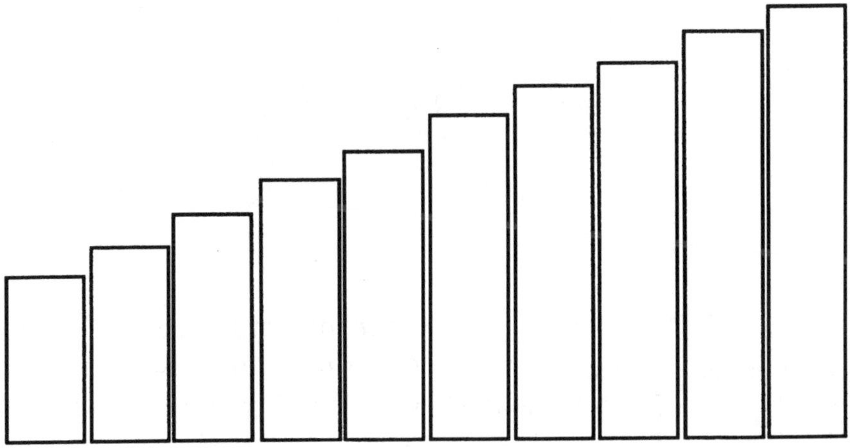

29

A riot breaks out in Ephesus – told by Demetrius the silversmith

Demetrius

Paul has been stirring up people, telling them our idols aren't gods. I used to make a lot of money selling silver idols all over town. After Paul spoke, trade began to fall off.

I called a meeting of the town's metalworkers and told them there was a danger of our business getting a bad name. Soon, there was a huge uproar throughout the city. It was chaos for several hours.

Eventually, the town clerk calmed the crowd. He reminded everyone that the people of Ephesus worship the goddess Artemis. Nothing could change that.

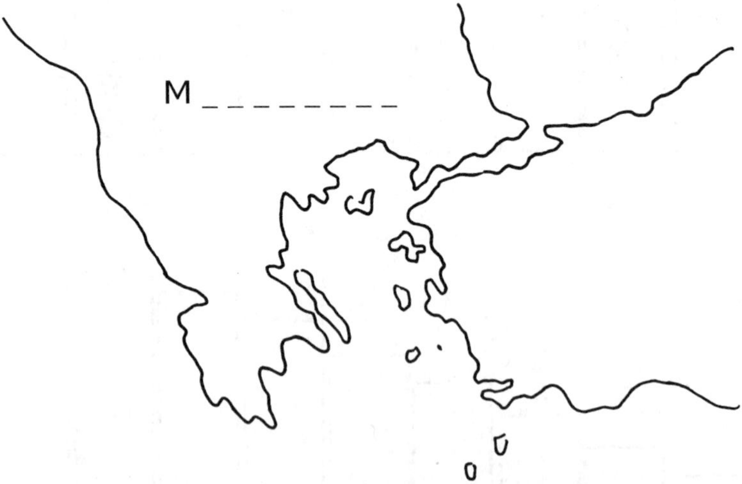

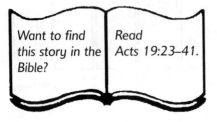

Want to find this story in the Bible? *Read Acts 19:23–41.*

After the riot where did Paul go? Look it up in the Bible (Acts 20:1) and write the name on the map.

30

The third journey continues – told by Luke

Luke

I'm Luke, Paul's best friend. After the Ephesus visit, a group of believers, including me, went with Paul to spread the good news. From Macedonia, we visited Achaia, and then Troas, where a young man, Eutychus, dropped off to sleep listening to Paul and fell out of a third floor window. We all thought he was dead but Paul healed him.

Paul was keen to reach Jerusalem in time for Pentecost so we hurried to Assos where we set sail along the coast, stopping briefly at Mitylene, Chios, Samos and Miletus. A few of us went on with Paul to Cos, Rhodes, Patara and Syria, where we landed at Tyre. On the way to Jerusalem, we stayed the night in Caesarea with Philip the evangelist, one of seven men chosen by the apostles to carry out the work of the new church.

While we were there, Agabus, a prophet, said that the Jews in Jerusalem would capture Paul. We were afraid for him and begged him not to go on. But Paul said he was willing to be imprisoned or even die for Christ.

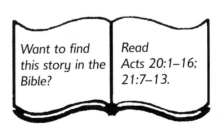

Want to find this story in the Bible? *Read Acts 20:1–16; 21:7–13.*

Who is this? He is in the story on page 53.
Join up the dots to find out.

31

Paul has problems in Jerusalem – told by a Roman commander

As soon as I heard about the riot in town, I ordered Paul to be arrested. However, Paul asked me for permission to speak to the crowd, so I gave it.

He went on about how he followed Jesus, the troublemaker we executed some years ago. I ordered him to be put in jail. But then I realised that he was a Roman citizen. That made me worried because it's illegal to hold a Roman citizen without trial. The following day, he appeared before the Council, where he insulted Ananias, the high priest. That was a bad move.

He went on to say he believed in people coming alive again from the dead. I gather the Jews known as "Pharisees" agree with him and the ones they call "Sadducees" don't. You should have heard them argue! They got madder and madder. I had to act – and fast – before they tore Paul to pieces. I ordered my soldiers to take Paul away by force and put him in the fort.

Solve the puzzle to find out what happened next.

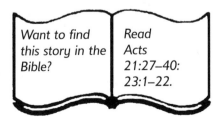

Want to find this story in the Bible?

Read Acts 21:27–40: 23:1–22.

See these pairs of letters? Write down the first letter of each pair. Then, when you come to the end of the letters, go back to the beginning and write down the second letter in each pair. Write the answer in the official report book.

PL AL UH LI SS NU EN PC HL EE WT TH OE LC
DO TM HM EA CN OD ME MR AS NE DN ET RP
OA FU AL PA LW OA TY BA YT TD HE EA JD EO
WF SN TI OG KH IT

32

Paul appeals to Caesar – told by Governor Festus

Festus

When I became governor of Caesarea, Paul had been locked up in prison for over two years. When I interviewed him, I was impressed. I would have released him straight away, but he'd already appealed to Caesar which meant he had to go to Rome.

Paul's trip to Rome nearly killed him. Julius, the centurion, described it to me when he got back.

"It was terrible," said Julius. "First there was no wind and we hardly moved. Near the island of Crete, an incredibly strong storm blew up. We were blown off course and tossed about for two whole weeks. Paul told me not to worry. He said an angel had promised we'd all be safe."

Can you spot eight differences in these pictures of Paul on the ship in the storm?

Want to find this story in the Bible?
Read Acts 25:1–12; 27:1–44; 28:1.

33

Paul settles in Rome – told by a Roman soldier

When the ship hit a sandbank off Malta, we thought we would have to kill all the prisoners to stop them escaping. But the centurion, Julius, told us not to. He wanted to save Paul.

I must say if I'm ever shipwrecked again, I'd like it to be on that island. The scenery was all blue and honey coloured, and the people were very kind. They gave us food, bandaged our wounds and invited us into their homes. We heard them muttering that Paul must be some sort of god because they'd seen a poisonous snake hang on his hand, but he didn't die. You can imagine what Paul said to *that!*

Even the island chief, Publius, invited some of us to his home. Paul healed Publius' father, who was very ill in bed with fever. The news of this healing quickly spread round the island. Soon there was a long queue of sick people standing outside Publius' house! Paul healed them all.

All winter we stayed on Malta. When we left, our new ship was full of gifts the islanders had given us. We sailed to Syracuse, Rhegium and Puteoli and at last arrived in Rome, my home town. Great to be back!

Paul was allowed to live by himself in Rome with a soldier guarding him.

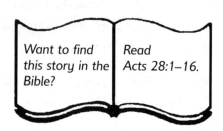

Want to find this story in the Bible? *Read Acts 28:1–16.*

Here is a map showing the names of five towns Paul visited. You will find all of them referred to in this book. Can you fill in the missing letters to complete them?

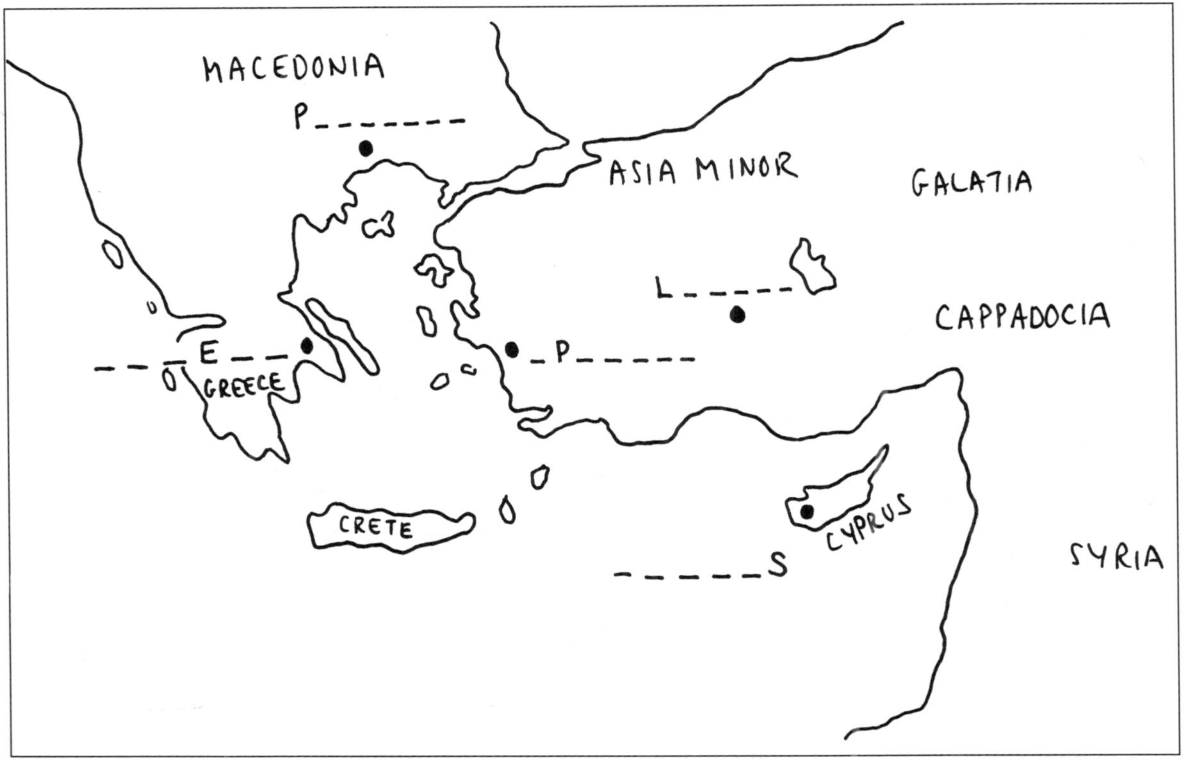

ANSWERS

Quiz

1 Raised his hands and blessed his friends.
2 Justus.
3 Speak foreign languages.
4 About three thousand.
5 The Temple.
6 An angel of the Lord.
7 Jesus, sitting at God's right hand.
8 Pray.
9 Baptise him.
10 He went blind.
11 He was baptised.
12 Non-believing Jews.
13 Tabitha was restored to life.
14 Animals and birds.
15 An angel.
16 Let Peter in.
17 A dark mist.
18 The Gentiles.
19 Timothy.
20 Hermes and Zeus.
21 Food and good behaviour.
22 Go to Macedonia to help.
23 They were put in prison.
24 Baptised the jailer and his family.
25 Berea.
26 To an Unknown God.
27 They were tentmakers.
28 He baptised them.
29 To Macedonia.
30 Be imprisoned or die.
31 Paul's nephew.
32 Malta.
33 He healed his father.

Puzzles

1 Jesus raised his hands and blessed his special friends then floated upwards to heaven. A cloud hid him from sight.
2 Matthias.
3 The apostles were filled with the Holy Spirit and began to talk in other languages.
4 *Please see illustration.*
5 The lame man stood up and started to walk. He went into the Temple, praising God.
6 The jailers found the prison cell empty. In the night, an angel of the Lord had set the apostles free.
7 "I see heaven opened and Jesus standing at God's right hand."
8 Simon asked the apostles to pray for him so that he would be right in God's eyes.
9 *Please see illustration.*
10 False/False/True/False/True.
11 Something like fish scales fell from Saul's eyes. He could see. He stood up and was baptised! After he had eaten, his strength came back.
12 One night Saul's followers took him and let him down through an opening in the wall, lowering him in a basket. *Please also see illustration.*
13 Peter sent all the mourners away, knelt down and prayed. Then he said, "Tabitha! Get up!" Tabitha opened her eyes and Peter helped her stand up. Because of this, many people in Joppa became believers.
14 God showed Peter all kinds of animals and birds. He told Peter to kill and eat them – but Peter argued. Jews have strict laws about what they can eat and the way animals must be killed.

"I can't eat those!" he said, "I've never eaten anything unclean."

"Don't consider anything unclean if I now tell you it's good to eat," said God.

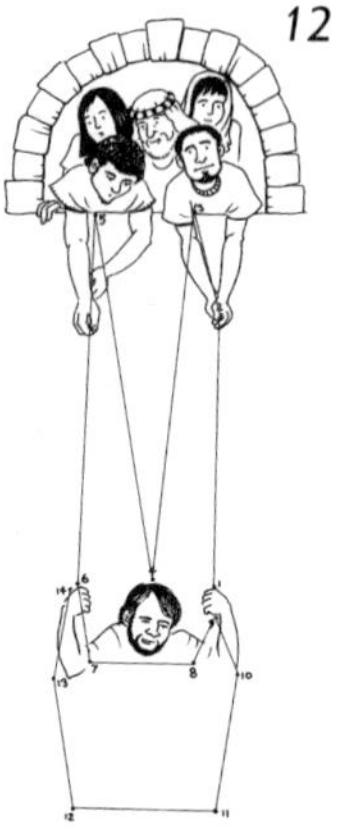

15 An angel woke Peter and his chains fell off. The angel led him through the prison gates to safety.

16 Rhoda was so excited she forgot to let Peter in! Peter kept knocking until the door was opened. He told his friends how God had brought him out of prison, gave them a message for the other apostles, and then went away to hide.

17 Elymas felt a dark mist cover his eyes and walked about trying to find someone to lead him by the hand. The governor was amazed and believed in Jesus because of Paul's teaching.

18 "I have made you a light for the Gentiles so that all the world may be saved."

19 Pictures 1 and 5 are the same. *Please see illustration.*

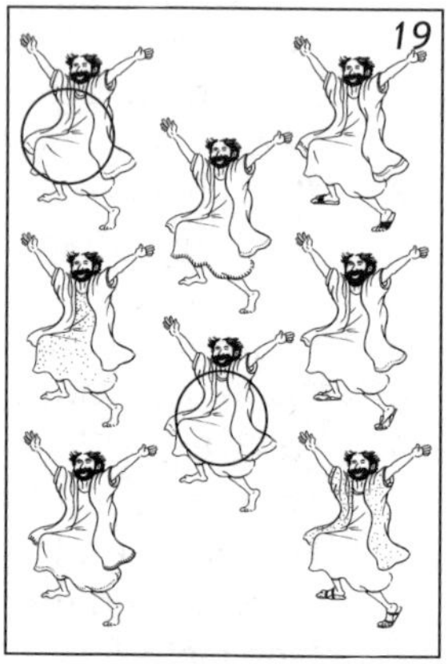

20 "We must pass through many troubles to enter the kingdom of God."

21 James said "Gather round and listen to me.
The words of the prophets all agree
With Peter's words. So let's write a letter
Telling those Gentiles they had better
Keep just a few of the Jewish laws
About behaviour and food because
That'll keep us happy – and Jesus, too –
So that is all they'll have to do,
As long as they're all baptised in love
And worship only our God above."

22 Paul had a vision in his sleep. A man was begging him, "Come to Macedonia and help us."

23

P	F	O	R	T	U	N	E
R	U	T	O	R	O	B	U
I	R	B	M	O	N	E	Y
S	I	L	A	S	L	A	P
O	O	E	N	M	A	T	A
N	U	K	S	E	R	E	U
S	S	L	A	V	E	N	L

The charge against Paul and Silas was that they were TROUBLEMAKERS.

24 *Please see illustration.*

25 Jesus is the Messiah.

26 "God, who made the world and everything in it, is Lord of heaven and earth."

28 Paul baptised them and they were given the Holy Spirit.

29 Macedonia.

30 *Please see illustration.*

31 Paul's nephew told the commander of a plot by the Jews to kill his uncle. The commander sent Paul away at dead of night.

32 *Please see illustration.*

33 Philippi, Lystra, Ephesus, Paphos and Athens.

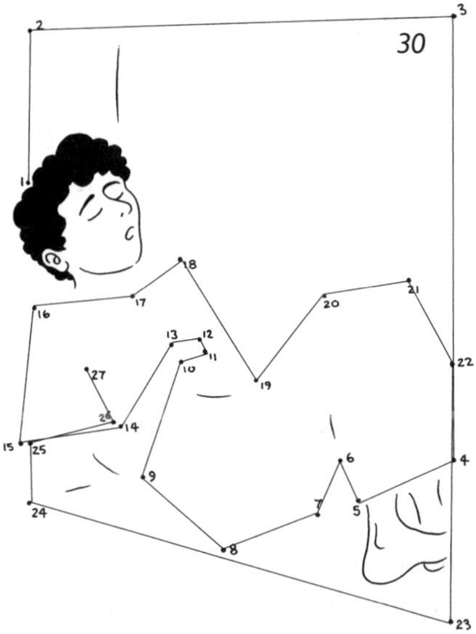

If you want to know more about becoming a follower of Jesus, you can read...

Me +Jesus and *Jesus=Friendship forever* are booklets to help you when you decide to become one of Jesus' friends. Easy to read, with zany pictures, they cost 99p each.

If you enjoyed reading your Bible, why not read a bit every day? *Snapshots* is a booklet to help adventurers like you to hear God's message to you as you read the Bible. Full of fun, puzzles and prayer ideas, it comes out every three months. £2.50.

10 Rulz will give you a whole new way of looking at Moses and the Ten Commandments – cartoons that will make you laugh and stories about some of the horrible things people in the Bible shouldn't have done to each other! £4.99.

Prices correct at the time of going to print.